FRANK LLOYD WRIGHT

Other Badger Biographies

FRANK LLYOD WRIGHT AND HIS

New American Architecture

Bob Kann

Wisconsin Historical Society Press

Published by the Wisconsin Historical Society Press
Publishers since 1855

© 2010 by the State Historical Society of Wisconsin

For permission to reuse material from *Frank Lloyd Wright and His New American Architecture*, ISBN 978-0-87020-441-8, please access www.copyright.com or contact the Copyright Clearance Center, Inc. (CCC), 222 Rosewood Drive, Danvers, MA 01923, 978-750-8400. CCC is a not-for-profit organization that provides licenses and registration for a variety of users.

wisconsinhistory.org

Photographs identified with WHi or WHS are from the Society's collections; address requests to reproduce these photos to the Visual Materials Archivist at Wisconsin Historical Society, 816 State Street, Madison, WI 53706.

Printed in the United States of America
Designed by Jill Bremigan

14 13 12 11 10   1 2 3 4 5

Library of Congress Cataloging-in-Publication Data

Kann, Bob.
  Frank Lloyd Wright and his new American architecture / Bob Kann.—1st ed.
      p. cm.—(Badger biographies)
  Includes bibliographical references and index.
  ISBN 978-0-87020-441-8
  1. Wright, Frank Lloyd, 1867-1959—Juvenile literature. 2. Architects—United States—Biography—Juvenile literature. I. Wright, Frank Lloyd, 1867-1959. II. Title.
  NA737.W7K26 2010
  720.92—dc22
                                    2009031170

Front cover: WHi Image ID 1921
Back cover: WHi Image ID 26558

Publication was made possible, in part, by gifts from Mrs. Harvey E. Vick of Milwaukee, Wisconsin, and from the friends of Ellen Nicolaus Purcell, in her honor. Additional funding was provided by grants from the Amy Louise Hunter and Alice E. Smith fellowship funds.

Contents

1

Thinking Like an Architect

Imagine that you are looking at an empty piece of land. You have been chosen to build a building on that land. It could be a home, a school, a hotel, a museum, or even a tree house. What would your building look like?

Architects are the people who plan and **design** buildings; they make sure they are built well and safely to last a long time. Before a building is built, architects often ask many questions to decide how to plan the building, including these:

❋ What do I need to learn about the people who live and work here?

❋ What do I need to know about this place to be able to make the building belong here?

❋ What is the **purpose** of the building? Who will use it? Will it be a school where children can learn? An office where people will work? A home where people will live?

architect (**ahr** kuh tekt): someone who designs buildings and checks that they are built properly
design: to draw something that could be built or made   **purpose**: goal or aim

1

⊛ What are the desires of the **client** who wants the building to be built?

⊛ What will make people who spend time in the building feel special?

⊛ What are the best building materials to use for the building?

⊛ What shape will this building be? How would a **blueprint** look?

⊛ Which colors are best for the outside and the inside of the building?

⊛ How many rooms will there be, how large will they be, and how high will the ceilings be?

⊛ Do the rooms inside need to be dark or light? How many windows will the building need to have to have enough light, and what sizes and shapes should the windows be?

Frank Lloyd Wright was an architect who designed buildings that were very different from other buildings. These buildings were so beautiful, and so **unique**, that people from all over the world continue to visit them. Many of his buildings were full of surprises and didn't look like anything people had seen before.

client (klı uhnt): a customer; a person or group that uses the services of an architect, lawyer, accountant, or other professional   blueprint: a detailed plan for a project or an idea, usually on blue paper
unique (yoo neek): the only one of its kind

This book is the story of Frank Lloyd Wright and some of the buildings he designed. During his 72 years as an architect, he drew plans for almost every kind of building: houses, hotels, hospitals, skyscrapers, schools, funeral homes, **planetariums**, museums, gift shops, stores, offices, banks, universities, theaters, parking garages, bridges, churches, **synagogues**, and gas stations.

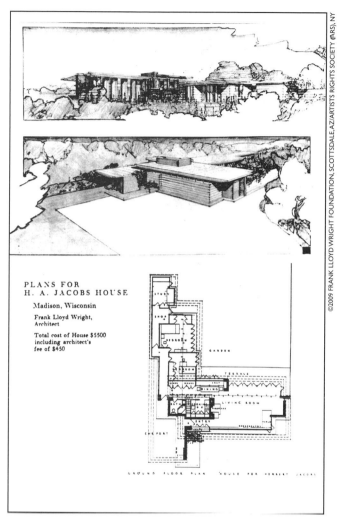

PLANS FOR
H. A. JACOBS HOUSE

Madison, Wisconsin

Frank Lloyd Wright,
Architect

Total cost of House $5500
including architect's
fee of $450

Architects make drawings like this as they work on the design of a building. You'll read more about the house in this drawing—the Jacobs House in Madison, Wisconsin—in chapter 12.

planetariums (plan uh **ter** ee uhmz): buildings with special equipment for showing movements of planets, stars, sun, and moon   **synagogues** (**sin** uh gogz): places of Jewish worship

Frank wanted to invent a new American style of architecture that made people feel free. Many of his clients and thousands of visitors to his buildings believe that he accomplished this by the way he opened up space inside of buildings and the way his buildings fit in with the natural **environment** or the **urban** space around them.

Frank's creations often were called "built experiments." He loved to try new ways to build buildings and use the materials for those buildings. Most of the time the results led to some of the most beautiful buildings ever built. At other times, cracks appeared in some of the walls, and the roofs leaked in those same buildings.

As you read about Frank Lloyd Wright and his buildings, look around wherever you are and imagine that you are an architect about to design buildings. How would you design your own home, your school, your library, your local grocery store, or even your tree house?

environment: the natural world of lands, waters, and air   **urban** (**ur** buhn): to do with or living in a city

2

Romeo and Juliet

In 1896, Frank's aunts Nell and Jennie Lloyd Jones needed water for their Hillside Home School in Spring Green, Wisconsin. Nine years earlier, Frank had designed that very school for them, and they now wanted him to design a **windmill** to pump water to the school building.

Frank's Aunt Nell played an important role in his life. She believed that Frank would one day become a great architect.

The biggest problem Frank faced was the strong southwest winds and storms that often came to Spring Green. He had to build a windmill that could survive violent storms. He designed a wooden windmill with

windmill: a machine operated by wind power that is used to pump water or generate electricity

2 towers, connected by thin strips of wood. He called the windmill "Romeo and Juliet." The 56-foot Romeo tower had a diamond shape that would split the wind when it struck. This diamond shape would help break the wind's power. The shorter octagonal, or 8-sided, Juliet tower wraps halfway around the diamond-shaped Romeo tower. This combination made the towers stronger together than if they were separate.

When Frank sent his design for the windmill to his aunts, they liked it. They showed it to their brothers whose farms surrounded the school. All of his uncles thought Frank's idea for 2 towers was foolish. They predicted that the first storm would blow the windmill over. They tried to convince the aunts to build a steel windmill like all the other windmills in the area. When the aunts **telegraphed** these comments to Frank in Chicago, he replied, "Build it!" He told them, "I am afraid all of my uncles themselves may be gone before Romeo and Juliet."

Aunt Nell and Aunt Jennie trusted Frank. The aunts had the windmill built just as Frank planned it, even though it cost them $675 more than a steel windmill would have cost.

telegraphed: sent a message by telegraph, or code, via electrical wire

When the windmill was finished, the aunts loved it. After each storm, the uncles would look out their farmhouse doors expecting Romeo and Juliet to have fallen. It never did. It's still standing today, more than 100 years after it was built. Frank was right; Romeo and Juliet outlasted his uncles!

Romeo and Juliet, the windmill that outsmarted storms, was one of a lifetime of creative ideas Frank came up with to solve **architectural** problems. Frank loved to experiment, and he wasn't afraid to fail. He said, "If you don't learn by your mistakes, you are not going to learn anything because you learn nothing from your successes."

When Frank was asked which of his buildings was his favorite, he answered that it was the next one he was going to

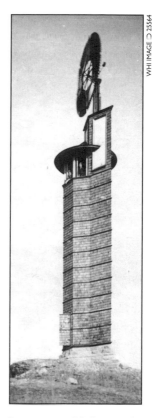

WHI IMAGE D 25564

Romeo and Juliet is the name Frank gave to this strange looking windmill, made of 2 towers, built to pump water to the Hillside Home School. *Romeo and Juliet* is also a famous play, written around 1600 by William Shakespeare, about two young people who fall in love. Why do you think Frank named this windmill Romeo and Juliet?

architectural (ahr kuh **tek** chur uhl): related to architecture, or designing buildings

7

build. He loved the challenge of figuring out new solutions to architectural problems. He found interesting problems in each new project, and he rarely solved a problem the same way twice. Frank loved to design fireplaces. Every time he designed one, he designed it differently from the others he'd created. In his career, he designed more than 1,000 fireplaces, and no 2 were exactly alike.

How did Frank develop into an architect? The journey began before he even was born.

3

Born to Be an Architect

How would you feel if your mother decided *before* you were born what you were going to be when you grew up? Frank Lloyd Wright said that his mother, Anna, knew he'd

WHI IMAGE ID 31680

grow up to become an architect. To encourage this, she hung wood **engravings** of **cathedrals** on the walls of the room where Frank would sleep as a baby so that he'd see beautiful buildings as soon as he was born.

Frank is about 2 years old in this picture. Already his parents had begun to teach him about art, music, and beautiful buildings.

Anna Lloyd Jones and her brothers and sisters moved to America from Wales in 1844. Many of them settled in a valley near Spring Green, Wisconsin, because

engraving: an artistic design carved or cut into a material   **cathedral** (kuh **thee** druhl): a large church

9

the rolling hills reminded them of Wales. The family **motto** was "Truth Against the World," which meant they believed they should fight for what they believed no matter what other people said.

Frank's father, William Wright, was born in Westfield, Massachusetts, in 1825. He was good at many different things. He was a lawyer, a minister, a superintendent of schools, and a music teacher.

Frank Lincoln Wright was born on June 8, 1867, in Richland Center, Wisconsin. He was one of 3 children born to Anna and William. He soon was followed by 2 younger sisters. William also had 3 children from his first marriage, so it was a lively household with many children.

Frank's middle name, Lincoln, was in honor of President Abraham Lincoln. But when he was about 18 years old, Frank changed his middle name to Lloyd. "Lloyd" was a common name in Frank's mother's family.

Frank's father taught him music. William wanted Frank to love music, but he was a strict teacher. He would hit Frank's

motto: a short phrase that states what someone believes in or stands for knuckles with a pencil if Frank was slow putting his fingers in the correct playing position on the piano. Still, Frank continued to love music throughout his life.

After he was born, Frank's mother, Anna, did many things to train him to become an architect. She arranged for Frank to take painting lessons because she thought it would help train his eye. She took him on long walks pointing out the patterns and colors in the wildflowers, rocks, and leaves they saw. She also bought a special set of **geometric** blocks called Froebel Gifts, which she was confident would teach her son about architecture.

Friedrich Froebel invented these blocks to spark children's imaginations. The Froebel Gifts were smooth maple blocks that came in many shapes and sizes. There also were brightly colored shiny papers for covering the blocks and little green pea shapes and straight sticks for connecting the blocks into simple **structures**. Anna believed that playing with the blocks taught children how to put together small things in order to build big things.

geometric (jee uh **met** rik): of or about the study of shapes   structure (**struhk** chur): something that has been built, such as a house or an office building

11

Frank loved building with the Froebel Gifts. Every night, he and his sister Jennie played with them. As his mother hoped, the blocks *did* make Frank interested in architecture. He later wrote as an adult, ". . . the smooth cardboard triangles and maplewood blocks were most important. All are in my fingers to this day."

4

Frankenrob and Cowpats

In 1878, when Frank was 11 years old, the Wrights moved into a home on Gorham Street near the state capitol in Madison, Wisconsin. The house had a big yard running down to the shore of Lake Mendota. Shortly after they arrived, Anna's brother James visited from Spring Green. Anna's other brothers visited often, too. They always brought presents from the farm: chickens, vegetables, barrels of apples, and honey. James gave the Wrights a gift of a cow so that Anna's children might have good fresh milk.

Frank was a shy boy. He spent a lot of time reading. He borrowed books from his father's library and from the Madison Free Library, and he received books as presents from his relatives. His aunts Nell and Jennie were his mother's sisters. They knew of Frank's interest in architecture and gave him *The Seven Lamps of Architecture*. This was a well-known book at the time and the first book he read about architecture. But his favorite book was *The Arabian Nights*, especially the story of Aladdin and his magic lamp.

Frank attended the Second Ward School. Kids teased Frank about his long, curly hair. They called him "Shaggy." Frank also painfully remembered that everyone in his class had to speak in front of the class once a month. He hated this.

Young Frank occasionally got into trouble. Once, during his middle-school years, he was sent home for dipping a girl's long pigtail in ink and printing a sign with it.

Perhaps the most important thing that happened during this time was that Frank became good friends with Robie Lamp. A childhood illness had left Robie unable to walk without crutches. One day, some of the other boys teased him, stole his crutches, pushed him down on the ground, and buried him in a pile of leaves. Frank later wrote that he chased the bullies away and rescued Robie. This began their lifelong friendship.

The boys shared many interests. They spent many hours together swimming in Lake Mendota. Both liked drawing, building, and inventing things. They built many toys for themselves, including kites, bows and arrows, and a bobsled. Because both lived close to the lake, many of their inventions were for playing on the water. They built a pedal-powered boat they called "Frankenrob" for summer fun on the lake, and they built their own ice boat for the winter.

Their favorite activity was experimenting on Frank's small printing press. Once they had taught themselves how to print business cards, they wanted a larger press. Although they couldn't afford a new press, this didn't stop Frank. He asked the father of his friend Charlie Doyon, to lend them $200 for the new press. Mr. Doyon agreed to provide the loan, if his son Charlie could share the press with them. So Frank, Robie, and Charlie formed a company called "Wright, Doyon, and Lamp, Publishers and Printers." Many wealthy people like Mr. Doyon would help Frank in the future.

Like many teenagers, Frank wanted privacy. His bedroom door had signs warning visitors that it was his "*Sanctum*

Sanctorum," Latin for "Private Room." Sometimes his younger sister, Maginel, would sneak into the room when Frank was gone. She later remembered his room smelled of printer's ink and oil paints.

Frank's mother began to worry that he spent too much time daydreaming. She decided she needed to make Frank tougher. When he was 11 years old, she cut his curly hair short and sent him to work during the summer at his Uncle James' farm near Spring Green. He spent the next 5 summers working at the farm.

As a boy, Frank spent many summers working on his uncle's farm where he grew to love the country.

Having lived mainly in cities, Frank was at first shocked by the difficult work that needed to be done on the farm. He had to get up at 4:00 in the morning to feed the pigs, milk the cows, and help in the fields. He hated all of these chores, especially taking care of the cows. He wrote that sometimes the cows "would lean over and crush the breath out of you against the wall of a stall. Beating them over the back with the milking stool only made them push harder." He grumbled about having to walk barefooted through fresh **cowpats**.

Frank had problems with other animals, too. He'd get pecked by hens, and they sometimes covered him with lice. He was disgusted when he had to cut off the heads of roosters and slit the throats of hogs.

Frank's back ached, his feet hurt, and his fingers were stiff. When he complained about the hard farmwork, his Uncle James would tell him to "add tired to tired, and then add it again." To Frank, this meant he could not use being tired as an excuse to stop working.

cowpat: cow dung or cow pie

17

Twice, Frank ran away from the farm. The first time, his Uncle Enos found him waiting to escape on the **ferry** across the Wisconsin River. His uncle told him to "work the soreness out by keeping on working." He had Frank feel the strong muscle on his upper arm and said, "Your muscles will be like that, Frank, if you keep at it."

Frank had many adventures on the farm. One way that we know about these stories is from his **autobiography**. Once, when he was 12 years old, he went barefoot to get a drink from the water jug at the edge of a field where he had been working. He took a swallow, put the jug down, and saw a rattlesnake. Its tail began to rattle, and its tongue began darting in and out. Frank froze for a moment. Then he grabbed a pitchfork and poked at the snake. Its head became stuck between two of the pitchfork's **tines**. Frank pounded the snake on the head with the heavy jug until he killed it. His uncle scolded him for fighting the snake. "Why didn't you get away from him? You are barefoot. You might get worse than hurt." But Frank just held up the dead snake and admired how long it was.

ferry: a boat or a ship that regularly carries people across a body of water
autobiography (aw tuh bı **og** ruh fee): the story of a person's life written by that person   **tine**: one of the sharp points on a fork or other tool

18

With each summer, Frank became stronger and found his chores easier to do. He began to enjoy life on the farm and to appreciate the beauty of the countryside. This love for nature helped him to develop his own style of architecture.

Frank learned many important lessons from working on the farm. As an adult, he'd often say, "Study nature, love nature, stay close to nature. It will never fail you." He became confident in his strength. He knew he could work long and hard without tiring. Even when he became a famous architect and was no longer doing farmwork, he still proudly called himself a "farmer."

The workers in this picture are hauling stones— a chore Frank did on his uncle's farm.

5

The Screams of Workers

When Frank was 16 years old, he saw something so horrible that he remembered it for the rest of his life. One afternoon, Frank was in class at Madison High School, which was located one block from Wisconsin's state capitol. The city was building a new addition on the capitol building. Suddenly, there was a loud crashing noise. Frank rushed to the capitol to see what had happened. When he arrived, he could see that the new addition had collapsed. Many workers were trapped inside. A cloud of dust rose through the air carrying with it the screams of the workers.

Frank leaned on an iron fence and watched for hours. He finally went home, but for several nights he had nightmares about what he'd seen. Eight workmen had been killed in the accident. Frank later learned that the architect for the project was blamed for the collapse. He was accused of poorly designing the columns that were supposed to support the new addition. He also was criticized for not carefully supervising the construction of the new addition. The **contractor** was blamed for using broken bricks and stones to fill the columns instead of the stronger materials he'd been told to use.

This experience taught Frank a lesson about the importance of safety and the power of architecture. Lives were lost when an architect did his job poorly. Frank never forgot this.

When Frank was a teenager, his father and mother divorced. Frank's father left home, and Frank said he never saw him again. With his father gone, Frank now had to help his mother support their family. He quit school and found a job working as an office helper and **draftsman** for Allan Conover, a professor of engineering at the University of Wisconsin. Conover designed and supervised the construction of many buildings, and drafting for him turned out to be a perfect job for Frank.

contractor: a person who agrees to supply materials or do a job, especially for construction work
draftsman: a person who draws plans or designs for buildings, using the architect's drawings as a guide

Professor Conover believed that his students and **apprentices** would learn best by working on real building problems. He gave his students and apprentices important responsibilities. Because Frank learned better by doing things than by reading about them, this teaching style was just right for him.

Frank was like a sponge soaking up the ideas about architecture. He learned how to draw blueprints of buildings. He visited many building sites and saw how Professor Conover solved problems. He spoke with the workers at the buildings and saw the problems they faced during construction. With his sharp mind and hard work, Frank learned quickly.

Frank soon became confident in his abilities. He heard that his uncle planned to build a **chapel** near Spring Green. Although he had worked for Conover for only one year, Frank sent his uncle plans for the new building. His uncle, however, hired a Chicago architect to design the chapel.

apprentice: person who learns a trade or craft by working with a skilled person   **chapel** (**chap** uhl): a small church

Frank also began to attend classes at the University of Wisconsin. Although he hadn't graduated from high school, he was able to attend the university as a special student. He'd attend classes in the morning and work during the afternoon. But he did not do well in most of his classes. He seemed to prefer actually working on plans or at job sites to studying. Later in his life, he was embarrassed that he hadn't finished his education, and he tried to hide that fact.

He did, however, enjoy the social activities at the university. He joined a **fraternity** and sang in a choir. He dressed in the latest college style: tight gray pants, fancy shoes with pointed toes, and a **mortarboard** with a **tassel**.

Although Frank's family was poor, his mother wanted him to enjoy university life. She sold her gold watch to pay for his membership in the fraternity. She gave him her special mink collar and sewed it onto his coat so that he would look good. Frank always was very conscious about how he looked and the kind of clothing he wore. He later became well known for his particular style of dressing.

---

fraternity: an organization of male students   **mortarboard**: a type of hat with a square, flat top
tassel: a bunch of threads tied at one end and used as a decoration on graduation caps.

Frank had little money, but this didn't stop him from spending. He charged fancy new clothes and shoes from stores. Throughout his entire life, he owed money because he always spent more than he had.

Even though Frank enjoyed the fraternity and singing in a choir, Frank grew **restless** at the university. He was unhappy in school and eager to move to a larger city. He told his mother that he wanted to move to Chicago to "begin to be an architect right away," but she wanted him to stay at home.

Frank still wanted to go to Chicago. He believed that he was going to become a great architect and that Chicago would give him the best opportunity to do this. The Great Chicago Fire in 1871 destroyed many buildings in the city. All this rebuilding meant there would be many opportunities in Chicago for someone interested in working as an architect. He also might have needed to leave

As a teenager, Frank was restless in Madison. He wanted to move to a bigger city with more opportunities.

restless: difficult to stay still or concentrate on anything

24

Madison because he owed money to some clothing stores. Frank secretly sold some of the valuable books his father had left behind and the mink collar his mother had given him. He used the money to buy a one-way train ticket to Chicago. His **ambition** knew no limits!

On a spring afternoon in 1887, when Frank was 20 years old, he took the train to Chicago without telling his mother. He arrived in Chicago with $7 in his pocket and the dream of becoming an architect.

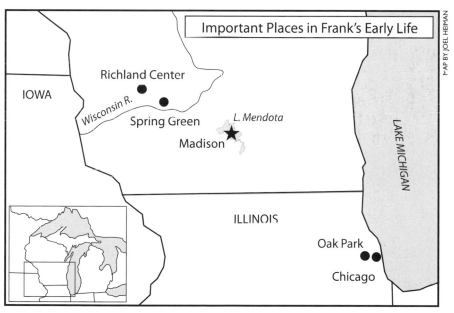

MAP BY JOEL HEIMAN

Important Places in Frank's Early Life

Richland Center

IOWA

Wisconsin R.

Spring Green

L. Mendota

Madison

LAKE MICHIGAN

ILLINOIS

Oak Park

Chicago

Much of Frank's early life was spent in Wisconsin and Illinois. Here are some of the places he lived.

ambition: strong desire for fame or success

25

6

Tired of Eating Bananas

Many surprises greeted Frank when he arrived in Chicago. In this very modern city, he saw electric lights, cable cars, and even a few of the new **skyscrapers** that were just beginning to be built.

Frank began walking toward the skyscrapers. The crowded streets seemed cold and gloomy. He found a restaurant and paid 70 cents for dinner. Although he now had less than $7, he spent $1 to attend a ballet performance. He rented a room in a cheap hotel and decided to save money by eating only bananas until he found a job.

After 3 days, Frank could not find a job with an architectural company. He was discouraged and lonely. He knew that he would soon be out of money, and he was already tired of eating bananas.

skyscraper: a very tall building

On the fourth morning Frank skipped breakfast. If he couldn't find work, he might have to return to Madison. He applied for a job at the office of J. L. Silsbee, the architect who had designed the Unity Chapel in Spring Green built for Frank's uncle.

Frank was interviewed by Cecil Corwin, Silsbee's head draftsman. Frank showed Cecil his drawings. Cecil liked them and brought them into Mr. Silsbee's office. Mr. Silsbee also liked them. He hired Frank for $8 a week.

Chicago was a busy, crowded place when Frank moved there in the late 1880s. After the Great Chicago Fire in 1871—which destroyed 18,000 buildings and left most Chicagoans temporarily without a home— there was much building to be done, as you can see in the top picture. This made Chicago a good place for a young architect to begin his career.

Cecil offered to treat Frank to lunch. The young men quickly became friends. They discovered they shared a love of music, books, and architecture. When Frank described the cheap hotel where he was staying, Cecil invited Frank to live with him in his parents' home until Frank found a better place to live. He promised Frank "musical" evenings around his new grand piano.

After only a year in Chicago, Frank was able to get a job with the best-known architecture company, Adler and Sullivan. Frank was very talented as a draftsman. He was also confident, as you can see in his expression in this photo.

That night Frank was eager to write a letter to his mother telling her about his new job. He asked Cecil if he could borrow $10 to send to his mother. He promised to pay it back $2 each week. Cecil agreed. Frank felt that a weight had been lifted off of his heart. He had helped his mother, found a job, and made a friend.

Frank began working for Mr. Silsbee as a **tracer**. Before long, Silsbee recognized Frank's talents and promoted him to draftsman.

One of Frank's first projects for Mr. Silsbee was to design a school building in Wisconsin. In 1886 his aunts Nell and Jane had established the Hillside Home School on the family's farmland in Spring Green. Aunt Nell hired Frank as the architect for a new school building. This was the first building Frank designed. He began to sign his drawings "Frank Lloyd Wright, Architect."

While working for Mr. Silsbee, Frank developed a lifelong interest in designing homes. After one year on the job, Frank wanted a new job where he could continue to learn and earn more money. When he heard that one of Chicago's leading architectural companies, Adler and Sullivan, had a job opening, he hurried over to apply. Frank showed Louis Sullivan his drawings. Several days later, Adler and Sullivan hired him.

Frank immediately began to work on the drawings for building the new **Auditorium** Building in Chicago. Like

tracer: a person who copies pictures or drawings   auditorium (aw duh **tor** ee uhm): a large room or building where people gather for concerts or plays

Silsbee, Sullivan quickly recognized Frank's talents when he saw his drawings and heard his creative ideas. Frank soon received a raise and became the company's chief designer. He now supervised 30 draftsmen.

In his autobiography, Frank tells how several of the draftsmen in the office were jealous that he was promoted. They teased him about his clothes and long hair. They began to pick fights with him. Although Frank was only about 5 feet 6 inches tall, he was very strong from his summers working on the farm. He secretly took boxing lessons to learn to how to defend himself against the draftsmen. Frank tells of one fight where he was badly cut by a knife but won the fight when he knocked his enemy out with a **T-square**.

Shortly after Frank began working for Adler and Sullivan, he attended a costume party sponsored by his church. While crossing the dance floor, he accidentally crashed into "a pretty girl in a pink dress," and she fell to the floor. Only slightly hurt, she laughed. Frank said he was sorry and learned that her name was Catherine Tobin. He asked her out on a date. Before long, they were taking long walks, and he was eating

T-square: a T-shaped ruler

weekly Sunday dinners with her family. Frank's mother, Anna, tried to keep her son and Catherine apart because she thought Frank shouldn't get married, but this made him even more determined to be with Catherine. On June 1, 1889, they married. Anna **fainted** at the wedding.

fainted: became dizzy and lost consciousness for a short time

7

The House with the Tree Growing through It

After his wedding, Frank made a **proposal** to Louis Sullivan. Frank asked, "If you want me to work for you as long as 5 years, couldn't you lend me enough money to build a little house?" Sullivan agreed to the loan. He wanted to make sure Frank continued working for his company.

Frank bought land near Chicago in the city of Oak Park. His mother convinced him to fix up a small house already on the property. She moved in there with Frank's sisters. Frank built a second house for himself and his new wife.

This first home that Frank built had many things that he included in the houses he designed in the future. He located the house on the lot as far back from the street as possible to give his family privacy. He decided to place the fireplace in the center of the house because Frank believed it was the best place to bring family members together. He designed

proposal: an offer to do something, often in exchange for something else

wide, open rooms with as few **interior** walls as possible.

From the moment he and Catherine moved into the house, Frank began changing it. He used his home to experiment with the ideas he was developing about architecture. He tested different building materials such as brick and wood. He'd rearrange the furniture to see how it changed the feeling of a room.

Frank built himself a workroom outside the house, and wanted to connect it to the house by a passageway. But there was a willow tree in the way. Rather than cut down the tree, Frank built the walls and the ceiling of that passageway *around* 2 limbs of the tree. People in Oak Park came to look at the "house with the tree growing through it." Some admired it so much that they asked Frank to design new homes for them.

About one year after they married, the Wrights' first child, Lloyd, was born. Five other children followed during the next 13 years. Frank wanted the best of everything for his family. He bought expensive rugs, books, and clothing, and even a

interior: the inside of something, especially a building

33

horse. Frank continued to spend more than he had, and he was constantly **in debt**.

Frank's need to earn more money grew as his family became larger. During his evenings and weekends, Frank began to design houses for people who were not clients of Adler and Sullivan, even though he had promised not to do so. He designed 10 houses for clients without telling Louis Sullivan. When Sullivan found out about this, he was angry and told Frank he must do designs only for clients of their company. Frank thought he should be able to build houses in his free time. He was fired from Adler and Sullivan. He was now ready to open his own office.

Frank's first client, William Winslow, hired him to design a house in River Forest, Illinois. The outside of the Winslow House was so unusual that many people came to see it. The front door of the house created an **optical illusion**. It was lower in height than the two windows on either side of it. This made the door seem very small, even though it actually was of normal height.

in debt: owing money   **optical illusion**: something you think you see that is not really there

The roof had long **eaves** that reached 6 feet beyond the walls. These eaves made the roof seem to float over the house itself. This roof was more **horizontal** than the other houses in the neighborhood, which usually were taller and had high, pointed **turrets**.

Frank also used bricks, concrete, and **terra cotta** to make the Winslow House look different from other

The Winslow House has strong horizontal lines, as you can see in this photo.

PHOTO BY JIM FRAZIER, JIMFRAZIER.COM

houses. He used the combination of the browns, reds, and tans in the materials to make the house fit in with the colors of the earth.

Some people loved the Winslow House, while others made fun of it. Because of all the comments, William Winslow changed the way he walked to catch the train to work to avoid being teased by his neighbors about his home.

eaves (eevz): the part of the roof that hangs over the side of a building   horizontal: flat and running in the same direction as the ground   turret: a round tower on a building usually on a corner
terra cotta: a brownish-orange clay   35

Shortly after the house was completed, a lawyer who lived across the street from the Wrights in Oak Park asked Frank to build him a house. But, he warned, "We don't want you to give us anything like that house you did for Winslow. I don't fancy sneaking down back streets to my morning train to avoid being laughed at."

Frank also tried to get more work for his new business by entering 2 design contests. He won the first contest to design 2 boathouses for the two large lakes in his old hometown of Madison. He quickly drew up plans for both boathouses. The Lake Mendota boathouse had space on 2 levels for 28 rowboats. The Lake Monona boathouse never was built because not enough money was raised to build it.

Frank lost the second contest, which was to design a new public library and museum in Milwaukee. He did, however, enter those same drawings in the Chicago Architectural Club **exhibition** in 1894. There the drawings caught the eye of Daniel Burnham, perhaps the most famous architect in Chicago. Amazed by Frank's designs and impressed by what he saw of the Winslow House, Burnham made an amazing

exhibition (ek suh **bish** uhn): a large fair showing different products

In 1893, Frank won a competition to design a boathouse for the city of Madison, where he lived as a boy. The boathouse on Lake Mendota was the first of many Wright buildings in Madison.

offer. He told Frank that he would pay all of Frank's expenses for him to study at one of the finest architecture schools in the world in Paris, France, followed by 2 more years of study in Italy. In return, Frank would promise to work for Burnham when he returned to Chicago.

Frank turned down this offer. He didn't want to learn how to build in the **classical** European style of architecture. He

classical: in the style of ancient Greece or Rome

thought this style put people in boxlike rooms. Frank wanted to create a new form of architecture that would encourage freedom. He wanted to develop an *American* style of architecture.

Inspired by buildings of ancient Greece and ancient Rome, the Wisconsin Capitol is built in the classical style. Columns, a dome, statues, and the white stone exterior are details that give a classical look. Frank was not at all interested in designing in this style.

8

No More Little Boxes

Imagine a large box. The richer you are, the larger your box. If this box is going to be your home, you'll want rooms. You might divide your big box into many little boxes by building walls to create smaller rooms.

For those who could afford it, this was the most popular way of designing homes when Frank was a young architect in the late 1800s. This way of thinking about architecture had

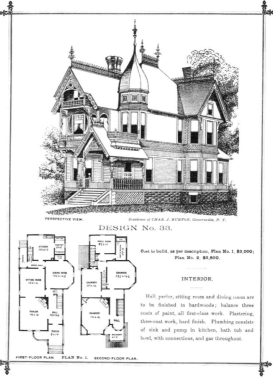

In the buildings that he designed, Frank was reacting to traditional American architecture of his time, like the Queen Anne house in this drawing. Queen Anne houses have many rooms and walls inside, and lots of decorations on the exterior.

roots in Europe. Frank wanted to develop a way of thinking about architecture that reflected the ideas and landscape of America. Some other architects working in Chicago at the same time felt the same way.

Frank thought dividing buildings into little boxes was ugly and made people feel as though they were prisoners trapped inside of jail cells. He wanted to invent a new American style of architecture. Frank believed that America was all about freedom: freedom to move, freedom to speak, and freedom to build strong families. How could his buildings **promote** freedom? His answer was to create the feeling in his buildings of being part of the wide-open prairie in the American Midwest. This new way of thinking about architecture became known as "the open plan."

Frank designed buildings in which the main rooms flowed together. He **eliminated** as many interior walls as he could to leave as much open space as possible. Many of the main living areas in his houses opened into one large space separated only by a huge stone fireplace. The dining room, living room, and entrance to the building all flowed together into one

promote: to help or encourage to exist   **eliminated** (i **lim** uh nay tuhd): removed

40

living space. There were no walls separating rooms except for the more private spaces such as kitchens, bedrooms, and bathrooms. When walls were necessary, they often did not touch the ceiling and instead were left open at the top. In the home he designed for his family in Oak Park, Illinois, his children loved to throw pillows and send messages over these walls without tops. It must have been like having a large volleyball net in their home!

Frank's buildings also included many windows to let in lots of sunlight and to make the outside flow smoothly into the inside of the building. This made the space seem larger than it really was. Many of the entrances to his buildings had low ceilings that led into rooms with high ceilings to make people look up and feel the freedom of the **vertical** space. It was as if they were looking up at the sky.

Frank and the Prairie Style

From 1893 through 1901, Frank produced 71 designs, 49 of which were built. Most of his work was for private homes in the Chicago area and in Wisconsin. He experimented with

vertical: in an upward direction; directly overhead

each of his designs as he slowly helped to invent a new style of architecture. This new approach to architecture came to be known as the Prairie Style because the houses were designed to **reflect** the flat prairie of the Midwest. Although Frank was not alone in this approach, the Prairie Style helped to make him one of America's most famous architectural **innovators**.

These are the main features of Prairie Style houses:

- They are built in a way that fits in with the natural environment or the urban space around them.

- Their shape is horizontal and low to the ground.

- They are built with stone, wood, and other local materials.

- They have large living spaces with rooms that are open to one another.

- They include many windows to let in natural light.

- They each have a large fireplace at the center of the home.

The Robie House is considered one of the best examples of the Prairie Style. In 1906, Frederick Robie, a bicycle manufacturer, wanted to build a house for his family in

reflect: to show or express   **innovator**: someone who invents something or does something in a new way

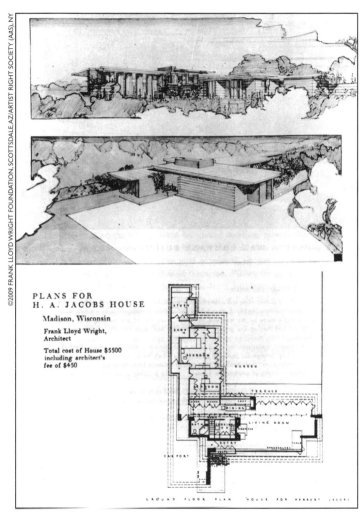

PLANS FOR
H. A. JACOBS HOUSE

Madison, Wisconsin

Frank Lloyd Wright,
Architect

Total cost of House $5500
including architect's
fee of $450

Can you notice the horizontal lines in this Frank Lloyd Wright drawing of a Prairie Style house? This is one feature of a Prairie Style house.

Chicago. He drew **sketches** of the house and showed them to several architects. They all told him that he wanted "one of those damn Wright houses," so he asked Frank to build him a house.

Robie knew what he wanted in the house. He wanted privacy, but he also wanted to be part of his neighborhood. He wanted to have good views of the city from one large sunny living area. He wanted

sketch: a quick, rough drawing of something

43

"all the light I could get in the house" and "rooms without interruption." He wanted a protected yard where his children could play. And, he wanted a garage.

The land Robie owned for the house was on a corner **lot**. Its long, narrow shape presented Frank with some interesting problems. The land was so small that the house filled almost the entire lot and left little open space around it.

Frank liked this **challenge**. The long, narrow lot gave Frank the idea of building a house shaped like a ship floating in the crowded sea of city people and buildings. Building the house in the shape of a ship made it feel protected from the closeness of the buildings surrounding it, just as a steamship's shape protects it from rough waters.

Frank and Frederick Robie quickly became friends. Cars were just becoming popular around 1906, and many people were afraid to drive one. Frank and Frederick, however, loved cars and driving. Frank had his own sports car that was nicknamed the "Yellow Devil." Frederick owned several cars.

lot: a piece of land   **challenge** (chal uhnj): something difficult that requires extra work or effort to do

The Robie House was completed in 1910. It was about 60 feet wide and 210 feet long. The front and the back of the house came to points like the **prow** of a ship. The neighbors nicknamed the house "the Battleship" because of its shape and because many saw the three levels of the house as the "decks" of a ship.

Look at this picture of a steamship and then look at the picture of the Robie House. What parts of the Robie House look like a steamship to you?

Look at this picture of the Robie House and name the features of the Prairie Style that it shows.

prow: the front part of a boat or ship

The roof seemed to float in the air. Part of the roof reached out nearly 20 feet from the closest support. To make sure people noticed this, Frank put plants below it.

Frank built the roof with **cantilevers**. Just as the strong base of a tree can support long branches, the Robie House roof was built with a strong steel **beam** that supported the weight of the roof that reached past the walls. These cantilevers shaded rooms during the summer but allowed sunlight to enter during the winter.

Frank loved the horizontal look created by the roof. To show this even better, he made it lower and longer than other roofs in the neighborhood. The roof became the most famous feature of the house.

Working in the Prairie Style, Frank made sure the look of the house reflected the land of the Midwest. The bricks at the bottom of the house were the yellowish-brown color of the prairie clay used to make them. The colors and lines of the house were meant to suggest colors and lines of the landscape of the prairie.

cantilever (**kan** tuh lee vur *or* **kan** tuh lev ur): a horizontal structure that has only one end supported, like a tree branch reaching out from a tree trunk   **beam**: a long, thick piece of wood or metal used to support the roof or floors of a building

The Robie House surprised visitors. The front door was hidden. At first, visitors wondered how to get into this odd house. If they kept looking, they eventually found the front door along a wall in the farthest corner of the house. The hidden doorway helped suggest the privacy that Frederick Robie wanted.

Once inside, there were more surprises. Visitors entered a dark entrance hall that led to a stairway with a bright light shining above. They climbed that stairway and were drawn toward that light. At the top of the stairs, they entered a huge, open room with only a fireplace to divide the space.

This idea of having one large room, instead of dividing a house into smaller "boxes" for a living area and a separate dining space, was a new idea in architecture. It gave people a sense of freedom they'd never experienced before. These more open rooms eventually became known as "open plan" designs.

Looking out from this second floor, the Robies enjoyed a fine view of the city. And they enjoyed less noise and extra privacy because the main rooms were raised one story above the ground. The bedrooms, even more private, were on the third level.

The inside of the Robie House was beautiful because Frank designed and chose the furniture; the rugs, lamps, plates, and silverware; and the color of the walls. Everything fit together perfectly to create one flowing whole.

Frederick Robie's cars were stored in a garage attached to the house. This may have been the first time a garage was attached to a house anywhere. In the early 1900s, many people still used horses as their main form of transportation. The stables were built away from the main house to keep the sounds and smells of the horses away from the spaces designed for people.

The Robie House had surprises for the children, too. The windows in a playroom came to a point so that the children felt as though they were on a small ship. They had a tiny garage built for their toy car right next to their father's garage. There also was a walled-in area outside where they could play safely.

Although some of the neighbors found the house ugly and complained that it did not fit in with the rest of the neighborhood, Frederick Robie loved it. He said, "I think it's the most **ideal** place in the world."

By removing the divider walls and making spaces flow together, Frank created a feeling of freedom in his buildings. Although he had made these designs for Americans, they **inspired** architects living all over the world. Look around your home; was it designed with more of an open plan or with smaller separate rooms? If you were building your own home, would you choose an open plan or one that divides the house into many small spaces? Why would you choose the plan that you chose?

ideal: perfect   **inspired**: influenced or enouraged someone to do something

9

"Something in Him Died with Her"

By 1909, Frank Lloyd Wright was one of the most famous architects in the United States. He soon had an opportunity that would make him one the most famous architects in the world. A **publisher** from Germany, Ernst Wasmuth, offered to create a book about Frank's work. Frank agreed to go to Germany to work on the book. It turned out to be one of the most important books about architecture ever published. The book contained plans of the buildings Frank had designed from 1893 to 1909. It was the first book of Frank's work to appear anywhere in the world. Now Frank was famous outside the United States, too.

When Frank was ready to travel to Germany, his wife and 6 children stayed home. While Frank had been developing his career as an architect, he had grown apart from Catherine and left her to raise the children.

publisher: someone who produces and distributes books or any printed material so people can buy it

In the meantime, Frank had fallen in love with someone else—Mamah Cheney. She'd been the wife of one of his clients. Mamah went to Germany with Frank to work on Frank's book. He believed he should be able to do whatever he wanted to do no matter how other people felt about his actions—or how his actions may have hurt others. He was *that* selfish. While Frank was a very talented architect, he did not always make good choices in his personal life.

When he returned to the United States a year later, many people were angry with him. They did not like the way he'd abandoned Catherine and the children. They did not like the fact that Mamah had gone to Germany with him.

Frank wanted to escape Oak Park and his problems there. His mother stepped in to help him. She gave him a gift of 31 acres of land she owned in Spring Green, Wisconsin, near other members of her family. Frank quickly moved to Spring Green and built a home for himself and Mamah.

Frank called this new home "Taliesin," which means "shining brow" in the **Welsh** language. It was the name of

Welsh: relating to the country of Wales

a famous Welsh singer-poet. The name also was significant because Frank built this home on the "brow" of the hill, just below the top.

Taliesin means "shining brow" in the Welsh language. As you can see in this picture, Frank built Taliesin just below the top—or on the brow—of a hill.

The hill had been one of Frank's favorite places as a teenager. He designed Taliesin to look as though it had grown out of the hill and always belonged there. Taliesin now stood over the beautiful valley where Frank had worked on his uncles' farms. He later said, "It should be *of* the hill, belong to it, so hill and house could live together each the happier for the other."

Taliesin became Frank's home for the next 48 years, but it was more than a home. It was a farm, his office, and a place to entertain clients. Like his Oak Park home, he used Taliesin as a place to experiment with his architectural ideas. In one bedroom, for example, he changed the way the ceiling looked 21 times.

This large fireplace is in the living room at Taliesin.

Frank and Mamah had lived at Taliesin for 3 years when a **tragedy** occurred. On August 14, 1914, Frank was working in Chicago. At Taliesin, Mamah's 2 children were visiting her. While they were eating lunch, a

tragedy (**traj** uh dee): a very sad event

53

newly hired cook and **handyman**, Julian Carleton, burned down the building. He then killed Mamah, her children, and 4 others who were there at Taliesin.

In Chicago, Frank received a long-distance telephone call telling him that Taliesin had been destroyed by fire with Mamah and her children inside. When he heard this news, he groaned. He grabbed a table to keep from falling. He immediately took the train to Madison, where his relatives took him by car to Spring Green. As he saw the smoke still pouring out of Taliesin, he heard about what had happened. Frank was heartbroken.

Julian Carleton was captured and put in jail. He died several weeks later. He never explained the reason for his crimes.

Frank missed Mamah terribly. His son John later wrote, "Something in him died with her, a something lovable and gentle that I knew and loved in my father." For a while, Frank returned to Chicago and lived alone. But he loved his Wisconsin home, so within 6 months, he began rebuilding Taliesin. He reused some of the stone that had been burned. He spent his days working on the designs. At night he played

handyman: a man hired to do various small jobs

the piano damaged in the fire or wandered the Spring Green hills.

During the years after the Taliesin tragedy, Frank spent much of his time in Japan building the Imperial Hotel. Maybe this was his way of dealing with the heartbreak. Also, it may have been easier for him to be away from the United States—away from where many people **criticized** the way he led his life. Despite his personal problems, his work on the Imperial Hotel made him even more famous around the world.

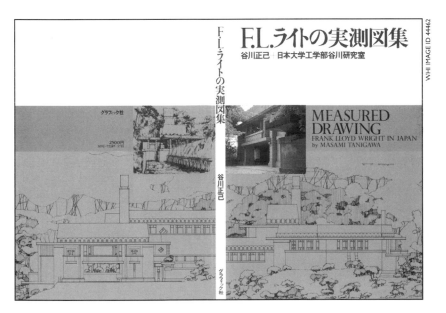

This book about Frank Lloyd Wright was published in Japan. His designs were becoming known throughout the world.

criticized: told someone what he or she has done wrong

10

Outsmarting an Earthquake

Imagine you're walking down the street when suddenly the ground starts shaking and buildings begin falling around you. An **earthquake** has struck. If you were to design a building in a place where earthquakes often occur, how would you make the building strong enough to survive them?

In 1914, the emperor of Japan wanted a new hotel to welcome visitors to the city of Tokyo. He chose Frank Lloyd Wright to design the new Imperial Hotel. Frank began work on the hotel in 1916.

The biggest problem Frank had was figuring out how to make buildings that would stand up during earthquakes. Many buildings in Japan had been destroyed by earthquakes. How could he build a 200-room hotel that would survive an earthquake? This challenge was even more difficult because

earthquake: a sudden violent shaking of the earth, caused by a shifting of the earth's crust

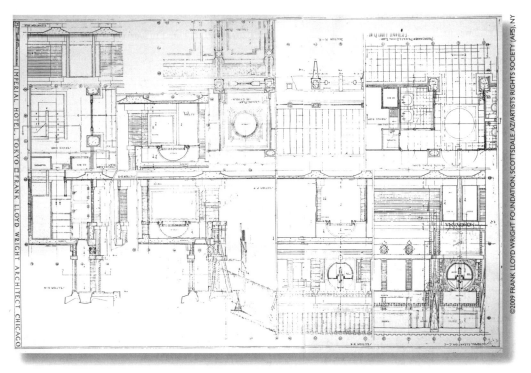

This drawing shows details of the Imperial Hotel in Tokyo.

the hotel would be built on land that had been a **marsh**. It would rest on 8 feet of spongy soil covering soft mud that was nearly 70 feet deep.

Frank studied earthquakes for 6 years. He learned that when earthquakes strike, they make the land move like waves in the ocean. Frank decided to design the Imperial Hotel so

marsh: an area of low, wet land

that it would be able to "float" on top of the ground during an earthquake as a boat floats on the ocean. He'd try to work with nature. Here was his plan:

1. He sunk the **foundation** for the building into the soft mud. He thought the mud would be a good **cushion** for the building and that the spongy topsoil would be a perfect foundation for floating the building.

2. He supported the floors of the building in the center, which is how a waiter holds a tray, rather than around the edges. This would make the floors wobble from side to side rather than break during an earthquake.

3. He made the building low—only 2 stories high—so that it wouldn't fall over as easily as a tall building might in an earthquake.

4. He built the hotel in **sections**, like the cars of a train, so that one section could break without pulling the whole building down.

5. He placed a pool of water in front of the hotel. This made extra water available in case of fire, because many Japanese buildings were made out of wood.

foundation: a solid structure on which a building is built   **cushion**: something that softens the effect of a disturbance   **section**: a part or division of something

Frank worked on the Imperial Hotel from 1916 to 1922. He traveled by boat across the ocean to Japan several times from his home in the United States. The voyage took 2 weeks each way, and he always was seasick.

Many people in Japan thought Frank's plan for the building was crazy. They were sure that the hotel would collapse and sink into the mud if an earthquake struck.

In April 1922, when the hotel was almost completed, a minor earthquake shook Tokyo. Frank was thrown to the ground, but the hotel had survived its first test.

This was the entrance to the Imperial Hotel. Can you see the reflecting pool in front of it?

The Imperial Hotel opened in 1922. One year later, the Great Kanto Earthquake struck Tokyo. It was one of the most powerful earthquakes in

Japan's history. More than 100,000 people died and 300,000 buildings were destroyed.

Frank was in Los Angeles when the earthquake struck. He wondered what had happened to the Imperial Hotel. A few days later, he was awakened in the middle of the night by a telephone call. A newspaper reporter told Frank that the Imperial Hotel had been destroyed in the earthquake. Frank refused to believe him.

A few days later, Frank received a telegram: "Hotel Stands Undamaged as **Monument** to Your Genius . . . Congratulations!" It was signed by Baron Akura, a representative for the emperor of Japan. Frank's clever design had saved the hotel. He framed this telegram and hung it on the wall of his office. He was very proud that his "floating hotel" had survived the earthquake.

After the earthquake struck, fires raged across Tokyo. The Imperial Hotel workers formed a bucket line from the pool to the walls surrounding the hotel. They filled buckets with water and wet down the walls surrounding the hotel, saving

monument (**mon** yuh muhnt): something to mark an important achievement

them from burning. Firefighters also used the water to battle fires in the buildings near the hotel.

When the story spread about how the Imperial Hotel had survived the earthquake, Frank became known throughout the world as the architect who had outsmarted an earthquake.

John Lloyd Wright's Famous Toy

When Frank Lloyd Wright built the Imperial Hotel, his son John worked as his assistant. Seeing how the beams fit together for the hotel's foundation gave John an idea for a new toy for children. He thought that kids could create their own toy buildings if they had the right materials to use.

John invented a toy that used small redwood logs of different sizes. Each log had **notches** on each end so that 2 logs could easily fit together. By combining different-size logs, kids could build houses.

Frank's son, John, got the idea for Lincoln Logs from seeing the beams of the Imperial Hotel, which fit together by notches. Ever since he invented them in 1916, Lincoln Logs have been a favorite toy for kids, with more than 100 million sets sold all over the world.

notch: a cut shaped like a U or a V

61

John knew he had a great toy, and he knew that he needed a great name for it. He called the toy "Lincoln Logs." Maybe he chose this name because the toys could be used to build buildings that looked like log cabins. President Abraham Lincoln grew up in a log cabin and was famous for chopping logs to build his homes. Perhaps because Abraham Lincoln was a hero, people would be interested in buying a toy named after him. John also may have chosen that name because his father's name at birth was "Frank Lincoln Wright." Or, it may have been because the word "Lincoln" sounds almost the same as "linking," which is how the toy's logs are put together.

Lincoln Logs immediately became a popular toy. Since they were invented, more than 100 million sets of Lincoln Logs have been sold around the world.

Lincoln Logs fit together because they are notched—just like logs in a real log cabin. The notches lock to make strong joints.

62

11

A School for Architects

Frank's personal problems did not end with Mamah's death and the burning of Taliesin. The 1920s brought other disappointments. In 1922, he and Catherine Tobin were

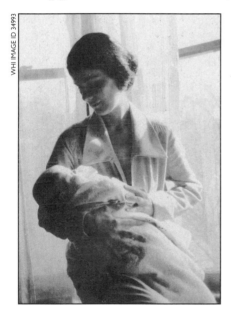

Frank and Olgivanna had one child—Iovanna—who is shown here with Olgivanna.

divorced; he then remarried and was divorced again. After Taliesin was rebuilt, a fire damaged it again.

But then he met Olgivanna Hinzenberg, who became not only his next wife but a driving force in his work as well. They were married in 1928.

Frank did little building during the 1920s. He lost several large

commissions for buildings. And the few commissions he received were not completed, usually because there wasn't enough money to build the buildings he designed. One of the buildings he designed that was not built was a cathedral in New York City that would have stood more than 160 stories high and could have held one million people.

Things became even worse for Frank when the **Great Depression** began on October 29, 1929. Several of the projects Frank had been working on were canceled. Like many Americans, he stopped earning money.

By 1932, the Wrights were in serious trouble.

Olgivanna and Frank were partners in life and work. Here, they are sitting together at Taliesin. Even during the most difficult times, Olgivanna believed in Frank.

commission: an agreement to do something   **Great Depression**: a time from October 29, 1929, into the 1930s when businesses did badly and many people became poor

Olgivanna begged Frank's sister for money to help them get through their financial difficulties. Frank was 65 years old, and most people thought his career as an architect was finished. But they didn't understand his amazing ability to think creatively at the worst of times. He wrote a letter to a friend promising, "I have my best work yet ahead of me." Olgivanna believed in him, too.

Although Frank couldn't find new clients during the Depression, he wanted people to know that he still was a great architect ready to work. He gave lectures at universities and wrote his **autobiography**. Many young people who read Frank's book wrote him letters asking if they could study with him. With Olgivanna's help, he started a school for architects. They called it "the Taliesin Fellowship." The school was located next to Taliesin on the Hillside Home School property, which his aunts had left to Frank when they died.

The Fellowship was very different from other schools of architecture. Frank's students learned by making things with their hands rather than by listening to lectures or reading

autobiography: a book in which the author tells the story of his or her life

books. This was
the way Frank had
first learned about
architecture from
Allan Conover. The
"apprentices," as
they were called,
studied architecture,
and they studied
sculpture, painting,
dance, and music.

Hillside School was one of the places architects-in-training lived at Taliesin. They also worked with their hands, growing food and chopping wood.

Taliesin was a
farm, so the students
also did farmwork.
Farmwork had
helped Frank
mature, so he
believed that kind

This is a typical apprentice bedroom at Taliesin. After working all day with their heads and hands, apprentices must have been very tired.

of hard work would help his apprenctices. He also needed
their **labor** on the farm! They milked the cows, chopped the

labor: work

wood, and grew their own food. They learned to work together because a successful architect had to be able to work with others.

The apprentices helped Frank with his projects. He taught them by showing them how he worked and by sharing his ideas about architecture throughout the day. The school was so successful that it continues to train architects today. Through one of the apprentices, Frank received a commission that led him to build one of the most famous houses in the world.

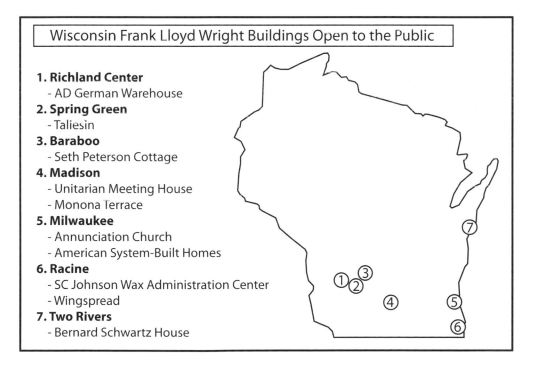

Wisconsin Frank Lloyd Wright Buildings Open to the Public

1. Richland Center
   - AD German Warehouse
2. Spring Green
   - Taliesin
3. Baraboo
   - Seth Peterson Cottage
4. Madison
   - Unitarian Meeting House
   - Monona Terrace
5. Milwaukee
   - Annunciation Church
   - American System-Built Homes
6. Racine
   - SC Johnson Wax Administration Center
   - Wingspread
7. Two Rivers
   - Bernard Schwartz House

12

The House That Floats through the Air

In 1936, Edgar Kaufman Sr. (E .J.) invited Frank to create a home on his 2,000 acres of land near Pittsburgh, Pennsylvania. His son Edgar Jr. had joined the Fellowship a few years earlier after reading Frank's autobiography. Edgar Jr. introduced his father to Frank.

Frank visited Pennsylvania. E. J. led him on a tour of his land to choose the best location to build a house. Kaufman pointed out several places where he thought the house might go. Frank suddenly asked him, "E. J., what's your favorite spot?" E. J. pointed at a huge boulder next to a waterfall. He liked to sit on the rock, listen to the **waterfall**, and watch the valley below. He and his family loved to picnic there and swim in the water below.

Frank began to imagine how a house might look at that very spot. He formed a picture in his mind of the rocks, the

waterfall: water from a stream or river that falls from a high place to a lower place

stream, the waterfall, the plants, the light shining through the forest, and the curves of the land.

He returned to Wisconsin and imagined how a house and nature could all fit together so that the house would really belong on top of the boulder E. J. loved. A house began to form in his mind that would be part of nature's music.

He decided to build the house right on the rocky **ledge** above the waterfall. The ledge would hold the house to the earth in the same way that roots hold a tree in the ground. The house would hang over the waterfall as the branches of a tree reach out from the trunk. It would look like a tree house floating in the air above the waterfall.

E. J. wondered what the house would look like and where it would be built. After 3 months, he couldn't wait any longer. When he was in Milwaukee on business, he called Frank on the telephone. E. J told Frank that he was on his way to Taliesin to see the plans for his house. Frank hadn't drawn any plans yet, but he invited Edgar Kaufman Sr. to visit him anyway. "Come along, E. J.," he said.

ledge (lej): a narrow shelf that sticks out

Frank's apprentices were worried that Frank had no plans. Kaufman was due to arrive in about 3 hours. Frank, however, hung up the phone, came out of his office, walked to his work table, and began to draw the plans. The design poured out of him. Talking quietly of his ideas while he drew, he said, "Lillian and E. J. will have tea on the balcony. . . . They'll cross the bridge to walk into the woods there. . . ." Frank wrote quickly without stopping, pencils being used up as fast as his apprentices could sharpen them.

Just before noon, Kaufman arrived. As he walked up the outside stone steps, Frank greeted him. "E. J., we've been waiting for you." He showed Kaufman the drawings for the house. They were amazing. The whole house was right there on the paper—the building, the trees and rocks, the waterfall, the colors, the materials. It was a house like none the world had ever seen before or since, and the basic plan never changed from what Frank had drawn in only 3 hours.

Frank designed the house hanging out over the waterfall so that it seemed to grow right out of the giant rock. Every bedroom had a white balcony that hung right over the waterfall. Stepping onto those balconies felt like being on a diving board above a swimming pool.

E. J. was surprised when he saw the plan to build a house right on the top of the waterfall. He reminded Frank that he had wanted to see the waterfall *from* the house. Frank

FRANK LLOYD WRIGHT, ARCHITECT. FALLINGWATER, MILL RUN, PENNSYLVANIANA, 1935. PHOTOGRAPHER: CHRISTOPHER RUDOLPH. COLLECTION OF FRANK LLOYD WRIGHT PRESERVATION TRUST.

Fallingwater, near Pittsburgh, Pennsylvania, is one of Frank's most famous buildings.

answered, "E. J., I want you to live with the waterfall, not just look at it." E. J. was convinced. When the house was completed, the Kaufmans loved it. Living with the steady flow of sounds from the waterfall, they felt that they were part of that waterfall.

When the house was finished, leaks and cracks appeared. Also, the part of the house that was built over the stream began to sag. Frank's plans for the house called for too little reinforcing steel, and the sag got worse over the next 60 years. In 2001, engineers added strong steel supporting cables to fix the sag and keep the building from collapsing.

The Kaufmans didn't complain. Many years later, Edgar Sr. said, "No **apologies** are necessary for what he [Frank Lloyd Wright] achieved."

Frank named the house "Fallingwater." It was so beautiful that it immediately became famous throughout the world. Many people believe it is the most beautiful home that's ever been built. Today, visitors from all over the world travel to visit it.

sag: to sink downward   **apology** (uh **pol** uh jee): an excuse or defense and regret for something that has been done

72

While he was working on Fallingwater, Frank won another important commission.

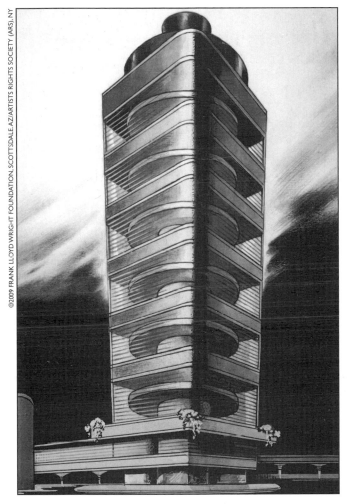

Here is a drawing of the Johnson Wax Building tower.

Herbert Johnson, the president of the Johnson Wax Company, hired Frank to build a new office building for his company in Racine, Wisconsin. Johnson wanted a building so beautiful that his workers would rather be in the office than in their homes.

Frank had an unusual idea to make the office special. He decided to support

73

WHI IMAGE ID 1911

WHI IMAGE ID 25943

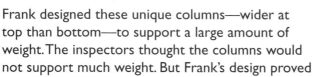

Frank designed these unique columns—wider at top than bottom—to support a large amount of weight. The inspectors thought the columns would not support much weight. But Frank's design proved successful. The columns were able to support 60 tons of weight—5 times more than they needed to for the building! The second picture shows how the columns were used inside the building.

the ceiling of the main workroom with white columns that looked like giant mushrooms. Each column would be 9 inches at the bottom and would spread out until it became 18 feet wide at the ceiling, which was 24 feet from the ground.

The building inspectors did not believe these columns would be strong enough to hold up the ceiling. Frank's plan had each column supporting 12 **tons** of weight from the ceiling.

ton: 2,000 pounds

74

The inspectors believed the columns Frank proposed would support no more than 5 tons. They thought Frank's plan was crazy because they believed that a column should be wide at the bottom and narrow toward the top. Frank suggested they test one of the columns to see how much weight it would hold.

A test column was built. On the day of the test, a crane piled loads of cement bags and gravel on top of the test column. All day long crowds of people watched to see how soon the column would collapse. When 12 tons were loaded on top of the column, it stood firm. Frank told the crane drivers to continue to pile on the gravel and cement. The column stood strong even when 60 tons of cement were loaded onto it. Finally, Frank ordered that the column be pulled down. The greatly embarrassed inspectors granted Frank a permit to use these columns. When the building was completed, the columns did successfully support the roof. The roof itself leaked, however.

Frank also designed a special 3-legged "tippy chair" for the workers. The chair would tip over if the worker didn't

75

sit perfectly straight. Frank thought this would improve the workers' **posture**. Herbert Johnson did not like these chairs. He asked Frank to design a 4-legged chair. After Frank sat in one of the chairs and fell down, he agreed to design a new chair.

Barkitecture

After building Fallingwater, Frank was so famous that he could have chosen to build only large houses for wealthy clients. Instead, he wanted to build homes for **middle-class** Americans. He designed a series of homes he called "Usonian," which may have been his word for "United States of North America." His goal was to create an artistic house that even someone who was not rich could afford.

Frank completed the first Usonian home in 1937 for Herbert Jacobs and his family in Madison, Wisconsin. Although he spent as little as possible to build the house, it was still beautiful. As soon as it was finished, curious people came to see it. So many people knocked on the door and asked to see the house that the family began to charge 25 cents admission for visitors to enter the house.

More than 100 Usonian homes were built during the next 20 years. Robert Berger, a schoolteacher in San Anselmo, California, used Frank's design to build one of these homes himself. After it was finished, Frank also designed an unusual second house for the Berger family.

Twelve-year-old Jimmy Berger had worried that his dog, a Labrador retriever named "Eddie," had no protection from the rain when he was

posture: the position of your body when you sit, stand, or walk   **middle-class**: of average income; neither rich nor poor

76

outside in the yard. Jimmy asked his father to design a doghouse for Eddie, but his father instead suggested to Jimmy that he write a letter to Frank Lloyd Wright asking him to design the doghouse.

Jimmy wrote that letter. He asked "Mr. Wright" to design a doghouse. He described how tall Eddie was, how old he was (in dog years), and other things he thought might be important for Frank to know to design the doghouse.

Nine days later, Jimmy received a reply. Frank said that he was too busy now to design the doghouse, but "write me next November," he promised, "and I may have something then." On November 1, Jimmy wrote again, "Dear Mr. Wright: You told me to write in November, so I am writing. Please design me a doghouse." A few weeks later Jimmy received 2 sets of plans for a beautiful doghouse. Robert Berger built the doghouse, and Eddie became the only dog in the world to have his home designed by Frank Lloyd Wright.

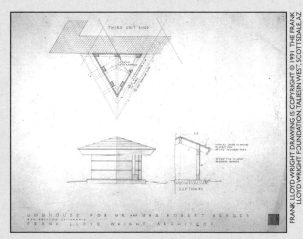

Here is the plan for a doghouse for Jimmy Berger's Labrador retriever. How would you feel if a famous architect designed a house for your dog?

13

A Flying Saucer or a Work of Art?

Frank's last major project was a museum. In 1943, Solomon Guggenheim hired him to build an art museum in New York City. Guggenheim wanted a building that would be completely different from other museums. Frank loved this type of challenge. He was so excited that he soon wrote a letter saying, "I am so full of ideas for our museum that I am likely to blow up."

Frank hoped to create a building that visitors would find as interesting as they found the artwork inside. Many think he did just that.

The Guggenheim is an eye-catching white building that is shaped like an ice-cream cone with ridges. There are no windows, so from the inside, the outside cannot be seen. This forces the visitors to concentrate on the paintings.

Entering the building, visitors see ramps going up in circles to the top of the museum. There's a skylit glass dome with light shining through to the **galleries** below. Some people say it feels like being inside the eye of a tornado.

An elevator takes visitors to the top of the building. They slowly walk down the ramps looking at the paintings until they reach the bottom. There are no separate floor levels. The walls that are holding the paintings are tilted gently back as though the paintings are at the same angles as the easels on which the painters created them.

Many artists hated the Guggenheim. They said it was difficult to hang paintings on the curved walls and awkward for observers to have to stand with one leg higher than the other to view the art. Other people disliked the outside of the building saying it looked like a flying saucer.

It took 16 years of planning, delays, and building before the Guggenheim opened in 1959. Neither Guggenheim nor Frank lived to see the opening. Guggenheim died in 1949, and Frank died shortly before the museum opened.

gallery: a place where paintings, sculptures, or other works of art are shown

Frank's design for the Guggenheim changed the way people look at museums. He wrote that he'd created a "beautiful symphony such as never existed in the World of Art before." As Frank promised, the building itself is considered one of the greatest works of the Guggenheim collection.

Some people think the outside of the Guggenheim looks like a flying saucer. Some people think it's a unique and beautiful structure. What do you think?

In what ways does the Guggenheim ceiling, shown here, reflect the outside of the Guggenheim Museum?

Frank was 76 years old when he began working on the Guggenheim Art Musuem. The older he got, the more energetic and creative he seemed to become.

He had designed every kind of building imaginable. He produced more than 1,100 designs, and about half of these were built during his lifetime. Frank designed buildings all over the world—throughout the United States, in Europe, and in Asia.

Frank had the busiest year of his career at the age of 90 when he received *40* commissions. A year and a half later, on April 4, 1959, Frank complained of stomach pains and was taken to a hospital near Phoenix, Arizona. Five days later, on April 9, he died.

At the time of his death, Frank Lloyd Wright was often considered the greatest American architect of all time. He changed the way Americans looked at buildings and the way architects around the world designed buildings. He received many awards during his lifetime including a gold medal in 1949 from the American Insitute of Architects (AIA), the highest honor possible to earn from other American architects.

Frank had strong opinions and liked to express them. What others thought about his work or his opinions mattered little to him. When he was asked how he felt when he saw an ugly building, he said, "It makes my teeth hurt." Shortly after TV became popular in the 1950s, he said, "Television is chewing gum for the mind." This meant that he thought TV was boring and a waste of time. In 1930, he wrote in a magazine article that if he had to choose only one living American who was a *genius*, he would choose himself, Frank Lloyd Wright.

Frank created a new American style of architecture in the way he opened up the space inside of buildings to make people feel free and in the way his buildings connected to the environment around them. Just as his mother wished before Frank was born, he wanted to be the greatest architect who ever lived. Many people around the world believe he achieved his dream.

WHI IMAGE D 6559

Some people retire when they get older. Frank chose to continue working. He designed three of his most famous buildings *after* he was 60, when most people are retired.

Appendix

Frank Lloyd Wright's Time Line

1867 — Frank Lincoln Wright born in Richland Center, Wisconsin, on June 8.

1878 — The Wrights move to house near state capitol, on Gorham Street in Madison, Wisconsin. Frank spends summers on his uncle's farm near Spring Green.

mid-1880s — Frank enrolls in classes at the University of Wisconsin–Madison; he works as office helper and draftsman for Allan Conover, professor of engineering.

1887 — Frank boards train to Chicago; he finds work at the J. L. Silsbee architectural firm.

1888 — Frank takes a job with Adler and Sullivan's architectural firm; he soon becomes the company's chief designer and begins work on Chicago's Auditorium Building.

1889 — Frank marries Catherine Tobin on June 1.

1890 — The Wrights' first child, Lloyd, is born.

1890s — Frank is fired from Adler and Sullivan; he designs houses from his studio in Oak Park, Illinois.

1890s — Frank—and other architects—work to develop the Prairie Style of architecture, which features horizontal lines meant to resemble the flat Midwest prairie.

1910 — *Wasmuth **Portfolio**,* containing Wright's design plans from 1893 to 1909, is published in Germany.

1911 — Frank begins work on Taliesin, his home near Spring Green.

1914 — Taliesin is set on fire, on August 14, by a handyman; Mamah Cheney and 6 others are killed.

1916–1922 — Frank designs and supervises building of the Imperial Hotel in Tokyo, Japan.

1922 — Frank divorces his first wife, Catherine, on November 11.

1923 — Earthquake occurs near Imperial Hotel—100,000 people are killed and buildings are destroyed, but the Imperial Hotel survives.

1928 — Frank marries Olgivanna Hinzenberg on August 25.

1929 — Great Depression begins, October 29.

1932 — Taliesin Fellowship (school for architects) opens.

1936 — Frank is hired to build—and completes—Fallingwater, his most famous house, on a waterfall near Pittsburgh, Pennsylvania.

portfolio: a collection of an artist's drawings or photographs put together as a book or folder

1936 — Frank is hired to design the Johnson Wax Administration Building in Racine, Wisconsin; the building is completed in 1939.

1943 — Frank is hired to design the Guggenheim Museum of Art in New York City; the building is completed in 1959.

1959 — Frank dies on April 9 in Arizona. He had created more than 1,100 designs in his lifetime; more than half of them were built.

Glossary

Pronunciation Key

a cat (kat), plaid (plad), half (haf)

ah father (**fah** THur), heart (hahrt)

air carry (**kair** ee), bear (bair), where (whair)

aw all (awl), law (law), bought (bawt)

ay say (say), break (brayk), vein (vayn)

e bet (bet), says (sez), deaf (def)

ee bee (bee), team (teem), fear (feer)

i bit (bit), women (**wim** uhn), build (bild)

ɪ ice (ɪs), lie (lɪ), sky (skɪ)

o hot (hot), watch (wotch)

oh open (**oh** puhn), sew (soh)

oi boil (boil), boy (boi)

oo pool (pool), move (moov), shoe (shoo)

or order (**or** dur), more (mor)

ou house (hous), now (nou)

u good (gud), should (shud)

uh cup (kuhp), flood (fluhd), button (**buht** uhn)

ur burn (burn), pearl (purl), bird (burd)

yoo use (yooz), few (fyoo), view (vyoo)

hw what (hwuht), when (hwen)

TH that (THat), breathe (breeTH)

zh measure (**mezh** ur), garage (guh **razh**)

87

ambition: strong desire for fame or success

apology (un **pol** uh jee): an excuse or defense and regret for something

apprentice: person who learns a trade or craft by working with a skilled person

architect (**ahr** kuh tekt): someone who designs buildings and checks that they are built properly

architectural (ahr kuh **tek** chur uhl): related to architecture, or designing buildings

auditorium (aw duh **tor** ee uhm): a large room or building where people gather for concerts or plays

autobiography (aw tuh bɪ **og** ruh fee): the story of a person's life written by that person

beam: a long, thick piece of wood or metal used to support the roof or floors of a building

blueprint: a detailed plan for a project or an idea, usually on blue paper

cantilever (**kan** tuh lee vur *or* **kan** tuh lev ur): a horizontal structure that has only one end supported, like a tree branch reaching out from a tree trunk

cathedral (kuh **thee** druhl): a large church

challenge (**chal** uhnj): something difficult that requires extra work or effort to do

chapel (**chap** uhl): a small church

classical: in the style of ancient Greece or Rome

client (**klɪ** uhnt): a customer; a person or group that uses the services of an architect, lawyer, accountant, or other professional

commission: an agreement to do something

contractor: a person who agrees to supply materials or do a job, especially for construction work

cowpat: cow dung or cow pie

criticized: told someone what he or she has done wrong

cushion: something that softens the effect of a disturbance

design: to draw something that could be built or made

draftsman: a person who draws plans or designs for buildings, using the architect's drawings as a guide

earthquake: a sudden violent shaking of the earth, caused by a shifting of the earth's crust

eaves (eevz): the part of the roof that hangs over the side of a building

eliminated (i **lim** uh nay tuhd): removed

engraving: an artistic design carved or cut into a material

environment: the natural world of lands, waters, and air

exhibition (ek suh **bish** uhn): a large fair showing different products

fainted: became dizzy and lost consciousness for a short time

ferry: a boat or a ship that regularly carries people across a body of water

fraternity: an organization of male students

foundation: a solid structure on which a building is built

gallery: a place where paintings, sculptures, or other works of art are shown

geometric (jee uh **met** rik): of or about the study of shapes

Great Depression: a time from October 29, 1929, into the 1930s when businesses did badly and many people became poor

handyman: a man hired to do various small jobs

horizontal: flat and running in the same direction as the ground

ideal: perfect

in debt: owing money

innovator: someone who invents something or does something in a new way

inspired: influenced or enouraged someone to do something

interior: the inside of something, especially a building

labor: work

ledge (lej): a narrow shelf that sticks out

lot: a piece of land

marsh: an area of low, wet land

middle-class: of average income; neither rich nor poor

monument (**mon** yuh muhnt): something to mark an important achievement

mortarboard: a type of hat with a square, flat top

motto: a short phrase that states what someone believes in or stands for

notch: a cut shaped like a U or a V

optical illusion: something you think you see that is not really there

planetariums (plan uh **ter** ee uhmz): buildings with special equipment for showing movements of planets, stars, sun, and moon

portfolio: a collection of an artist's drawings or photographs put together as a book or folder

posture: the position of your body when you sit, stand, or walk

promote: to help or encourage to exist

proposal: an offer to do something, often in exchange for something else

prow: the front part of a boat or ship

publisher: someone who produces and distributes books or any printed material so people can buy it

purpose: goal or aim

reflect: to show or express

restless: difficult to stay still or concentrate on anything

sag: to sink downward

section: a part or division of something

sketch: a quick, rough drawing of something

skyscraper: a very tall building

structure (**struhk** chur): something that has been built, such as a house or an office building

synagogues (**sin** uh gogz): places of Jewish worship

T-square: a T-shaped ruler

tassel: a bunch of threads tied at one end and used as a decoration on graduation caps

telegraphed: sent a message by telegraph, or code, via electrical wire

terra cotta: a brownish-orange clay

tine: one of the sharp points on a fork or other tool

ton: 2,000 pounds

tracer: a person who copies pictures or drawings

tragedy (**traj** uh dee): a very sad event

turret: a round tower on a building usually on a corner

unique (yoo **neek**): the only one of its kind

urban (**ur** buhn): to do with or living in a city

vertical: in an upward direction; directly overhead

waterfall: water from a stream or river that falls from a high place to a
   lower place

Welsh: relating to the country of Wales

windmill: a machine operated by wind power that is used to pump
   water or generate electricity

Reading Group Guide and Activities

Discussion Questions

⚜   Nature was very important to Frank. He once said,"Study nature, love nature, stay close to nature. It will never fail you." Give three examples of how Frank worked with nature to make his designs more beautiful. These examples can be names of Frank's buildings, details about his buildings, or even photographs of buildings from this book. Explain how you made your selections.

⚜   A number of strong women helped Frank believe in himself and his work. His mother, Anna Lloyd Jones, and his wife, Olgivanna, were 2 such women. In what ways did they help or encourage Frank? Give specific examples. Think of the people in your life who have helped you. In what ways have they helped you?

⚜   Frank and other architects working around 1900 developed a style of building called the Prairie Style. They used words such as *open* and *free* to talk about how the spaces inside the houses fit together and how it felt to be inside these houses. How is the Prairie Style of architecture different from the way other houses were built at the time? Explain which kind of house would be more comfortable for you. Why would you prefer living there?

⚜   Life is not always easy. Neither is learning to be an architect. Frank said,"If you do not learn from your mistakes, you are not going to learn anything, because you learn nothing from your successes."

What do you think he meant by this? Name 4 mistakes or setbacks that Frank experienced during his life. What do you think he learned from these? Describe a mistake you made and what you learned from it.

Activities

There are plans for various Frank Lloyd designs in this book—for the Jacobson House in chapter 1, the Imperial Hotel in chapter 10, even for a doghouse in chapter 12. Architects draw plans such as these before beginning to build. Think about the kind of house you might create for yourself. On a piece of graph paper, draw a plan for your dream house. Then, write a caption to describe what you visualize and why you made the choices that you did.

As a boy, Frank played with wooden building blocks called Froebel Gifts. Frank's son, John, invented Lincoln Logs in 1916, when his father was working on the Imperial Hotel in Japan. John designed Lincoln Logs to snap together and lock in place—like beams in the real hotel—to teach children to work with their hands and to learn about building. Ask your parents or an older relative about a toy they played with as children. What did they learn from playing with it? Write a paragraph describing the toy and what they learned. If the toy is available, bring it in to class. Or, describe a toy that has been important in your own learning and share that with the class.

In chapter 11, the author describes how Frank and Olgivanna started a school for architects at Taliesin. The Taliesin Fellowship had a unique approach to teaching about building. What skills did the students learn? What things did the students learn that did *not* relate directly to architecture? Why do you think Frank and Olgivanna were trying to teach different skills to the apprentices? What do you think Frank learned *from* the students? Put yourself in Frank's place. If you were starting a school for architects, what skills would you make sure your students learned? Make a chart. On the left side, write the skill, and on the right side tell why it is important for an architect to have that skill.

To Learn More about Frank Lloyd Wright and Architecture

Balliatt, Blue. *The Wright 3.* New York: Scholastic Press, 2006.

Casey, Dennis. *Stained Glass Window Designs of Frank Lloyd Wright.* Mineola, NY: Dover, 1997.

Fleming, Diane Breshan. *Simply Wright: A Journey into the Ideas of Frank Lloyd Wright's Architecture.* Castleconal Press, 2001.

La Fontaine, Bruce. *Famous Buildings of Frank Lloyd Wright.* Mineola, NY: Dover, 1996.

Malone, Bobbie, and Vivian Greblo. *Wisconsin's Built Environment.* Wisconsin Historical Society Press, 1999.

Mayo, Gretchen Will. *Frank Lloyd Wright.* Milwaukee: World Almanac Library, 2004.

Rubins, Susan Goldman. *Frank Lloyd Wright.* New York: Harry N. Abrams, 1994.

Thorne-Thomsen, Kathleen. *Frank Lloyd Wright for Kids: His Life and Ideas, 21 Activities.* Chicago Review Press, 1994.

Wright, David K. *Frank Lloyd Wright: Visionary Architect.* Springfield, NJ: Enslow Publishers, 1999

Monona Terrace Community and Convention Center, One John Nolen Drive Madison, WI 53703, Phone: (608) 261-4000. Designed by Wright between 1938 and 1959; completed and open to the public since 1997. Tours last 1 hour.

Acknowledgments

My home in Madison is less than one mile from Frank Lloyd Wright's childhood home on Gorham Street. I think about him whenever I pass the corner where his home used to be. We are fortunate to have so many reminders in Madison and throughout Wisconsin of Frank Lloyd Wright and the extraordinary buildings he designed.

In 1998, I developed a storytelling performance for the Taliesin Preservation Commission called "If I Were a Building: Frank Lloyd Wright and the Personalities of Places." This collaboration provided me with the rich opportunity to learn about Wright's life and work. It helped me to appreciate the built environment in ways I'd never considered. And I had the rare pleasure of performing in a theater Frank Lloyd Wright had designed. More than a decade later, the Wisconsin Historical Society Press encouraged me to write Frank Lloyd Wright's biography, which provided me with the privilege of revisiting his life and accomplishments. Once again, I found myself seeing the world differently in trying to look at the built environment through his eyes.

I am grateful to my friends, family members, and Wisconsin Historical Society staff for their invaluable suggestions and contributions to this book. Caroline Hoffman, Lynn Archer, Judy Landsman, and Deborah Waxman all helped to polish my language and enliven my stories. Barb and Don Sanford shared their passion for Frank Lloyd Wright's architecture and insights into his life. Jim Good provided his expertise in the questions architects ask when they're designing a building. Bobbie Malone, Director of the Office of School Services for the

Wisconsin Historical Society, contributed her wisdom and knowledge about writing a biography that would be both interesting and accessible to young readers. John Motoviloff, my editor at the Wisconsin Historical Society Press, made sure I offered a balanced account of Frank Lloyd Wright's personal and professional life; Kathleen Carey did excellent image research. Historical Society architectural experts, Jim Draeger and Daina Penkiunas, offered helpful suggestions on early drafts. Thank you all for your assistance.

Index

This index points you to the pages where you can read about persons, places, and ideas. If you do not find the word you are looking for, try to think of another word that means about the same thing.

When you see a page number in **bold** it means there is a picture on that page.